Rudolph Walker
OBE

A PROFILE

Verna Wilkins
illustrations by Debbie Hinks

Tamarind

Rudolph Walker – Black Stars
TAMARIND BOOKS 978 1 870 51689 1

Published in Great Britain by Tamarind Books,
a division of Random House Children's Books
A Random House Group Company

This edition published 2008

1 3 5 7 9 10 8 6 4 2

Text copyright © Verna Wilkins 2008
Illustrations copyright © Debbie Hinks 2008

Set in Sabon

TAMARIND BOOKS
61–63 Uxbridge Road, London, W5 5SA

www.tamarindbooks.co.uk
www.kidsatrandomhouse.co.uk
www.rbooks.co.uk
Addresses for companies within The Random House Group Limited can be found at:
www.randomhouse.co.uk/offices.htm
THE RANDOM HOUSE GROUP Limited Reg. No. 954009
A CIP catalogue record for this book is available from the British Library.
Printed and bound in China

Contents

CHAPTER ONE

On the *EastEnders* Set

THE QUEEN VIC LOOKED REAL. The whole street, as well as the streets around it, looked real. So did the houses and the market stall. The allotment was very well cared for and there was a gardener working between neat rows of zinnias with colourful blooms. In one corner of the garden towering above everything else, were rows of corn, swaying in the cool, mid-afternoon London breeze.

The allotment was the only real thing on that

Rudolph as Patrick Trueman and Angela Wynter as Yolande Trueman, in *EastEnders*

street. It was so real that the gardener picked two fat, ripe ears of corn and gave one to Rudolph and one to me.

That was real. The rest was a façade – wooden panels painted so they look like buildings. The Queen Vic was a flat front, with nothing behind it, and so were all the houses in Albert Square – just panels. This was the set, the exterior set, where all the outdoor scenes are shot, the place where actors work on location for *EastEnders*, the popular BBC TV Drama series watched by millions of people.

Gary Beadle as Paul, Rudolph as Patrick and Nicholas Bailey as Dr Trueman, in *EastEnders*

Rudolph as Patrick Trueman

"So where is the inside of the Queen Victoria Pub where everyone gathers for drinks and celebrations?" I asked Rudolph Walker, who plays Patrick Trueman in *EastEnders*.

"The indoor scenes are shot in another building not far away. That's another set, made to look like the inside of a real, old-fashioned English pub."

"What about the drinks? Do you have real beer and wine?" I asked Rudolph.

"Oh, no! Water with a bit of colour is all we drink on the set. No alcohol is allowed."

With a laugh as smooth as dark chocolate, Rudolph

jokes, "I'm real, for now, but soon I have to change into Patrick. I put on my old-fashioned clothes, my hat, my gold tooth and go on set to walk and talk as Patrick, husband to Yolande. This is how I earn my living. This is my job."

The dictionary definition of an actor is 'a person who pretends to be something he or she is not'. Successful actors can earn large salaries. These include some Americans, such as Will Smith, Samuel L. Jackson, Whoopi Goldberg, Halle Berry, George Clooney, Cuba Gooding Jr. and others. However, hundreds of actors spend time 'resting' while they wait for the next job.

Rudolph as barrister Larry Scott, in *Black Silk*, a drama series about a lawyer in London

4

CHAPTER TWO

Acting as Work

AN INTERVIEW WITH RUDOLPH WALKER:

Q: Who are the script writers for *EastEnders*?

A: Many people work as script writers on the programme. They have a variety of professional backgrounds and they come to the show with a great deal of knowledge about the characters and past storylines.

Q: Do the actors get a say in how a character would behave?

A: Sometimes. I read the scripts for my character and sometimes make suggestions.

Q: How does rehearsing for TV differ from rehearsing a play for the theatre?

A: There are no rehearsals for TV. The actors should already know their lines when they arrive on the set. The director and all the actors in the particular scene get together and run through the lines in about 10 minutes.

Then comes blocking. The cameras are put into place. Then the director decides on the actors' positions – where they enter the set, where they stand, how they move for the best effect and which camera angles will be used.

The term blocking comes from the fact that years ago, theatre directors would work these details out on a model of the stage. They used small blocks of wood in place of the actors.

After blocking, there's one more run through with the cameras in place. There's time for a second run for any changes that need doing. Then comes the final take, which is the actual recording.

Diane Parish as Denise Wicks with Rudolph
as Patrick Trueman, in *EastEnders*

Barbara Windsor as Peggy Mitchell, Rudolph as
Patrick Trueman and Angela Wynter as Yolande,
at the opening of Patrick's car lot, in *EastEnders*

Q: How many episodes do they record at a time?
A: In one day I can record 4 episodes. But this varies
greatly.

Q: How did you get the part?
A: I was head hunted. Someone suggested me for
the role and then someone from the production
company approached me.

Q: Are you happy at *EastEnders*?
A: Yes, I am.

Q: Do you have friends among the *EastEnders* cast?
A: We are all friends. We get on well with each other.

Q: What are the good things about being a star?
A: I can influence people positively. I'm invited to speak at functions and can use my name to make a positive difference to disadvantaged groups. Also it's great to be doing something that I really enjoy.

Q: What are the negative things about your job?
A: It's not easy to keep my privacy.

Rudolph delivering the keynote speech at
CRE Race in the Media Awards, 1993

CHAPTER THREE

Early Years

RUDOLPH MALCOLM WALKER was born on 28th September 1939, at 10 Tenth Street, San Juan in Trinidad, a beautiful island in the Caribbean.

As a young child, everyone called him Malcolm. To this day, his family and old school friends call him Malcolm. His close family consisted of his mother and two younger sisters. There was an extended family – uncles, aunts and cousins – many of whom supported Rudolph throughout his early years in Trinidad.

His family was poor, but there was always enough food. In the small garden that surrounded his home grew mangoes and plums, yam and bananas. Malcolm's mother also kept chickens. These provided eggs and meat.

Rudolph's home had only two rooms. A beautiful four poster bed with a brass frame half filled the bedroom. Beside the bed was a small bamboo table with a lace cover. In the living room, there was an old rocking chair, with two other chairs and a table nearby.

Like many other houses in San Juan at that time, there was no electricity. Rudolph did his homework at night in the living room, dimly lit by a kerosene lamp or candles. There was no running water. Every morning, before his 20-minute walk to school, Rudolph fetched several buckets of water from a roadside standpipe for cooking and washing.

Most of the families in his neighbourhood were poor. The children received very few presents, or none at all, at Christmas and on birthdays. So they made their own toys.

The boys made boats by peeling chunks of bark off trees. They had to work carefully so that the bark didn't split and kept its natural curve. They rubbed candle wax on the outside of the boats to help them travel faster.

They sailed these boats along the open drains and canals in the rainy season when the water sped downhill swiftly. The competition was intense and some terrific races took place. Malcolm was very competitive and usually had a winning boat.

CHAPTER FOUR

Island Pastimes

KITE SEASON was one the great highlights of the year. The children in villages all over Trinidad made their own kites. They stripped the large leaves off coconut trees and made the frames for the kites from the strong spines of the leaves. They then covered the frames with brightly-coloured tissue paper.

During the kite season, the sky above San Juan and the other towns and villages in Trinidad was alive with spectacular kites. They flew high in the air, their long, colourful tails made of bits of old rags.

Rudolph aged 5

Once, when he was making a tail for his kite, Malcolm found himself in terrible trouble.

He picked up what he thought was an old skirt. It was bright red. He shredded it into strips and made a beautiful tail for the kite.

"I hope, Malcolm," said his mother angrily, holding up what was left of her favourite skirt, "that this is not what I think it is!"

Malcolm ran off, clutching his kite, hoping that she would soon calm down. Later on, he sneaked back into the house when his mother was too busy to notice him.

That kite was one of the best he had ever made. He had spent hours sticking razors to the tail so that it would cut the strings of the competition as dozens of kites ducked, dived and criss-crossed in the air.

From then on, Malcolm was more careful and made his kite tails from old typewriter ribbons.

13

Everybody in Trinidad enjoyed cricket and followed the West Indies Cricket Team, which has a glorious history.

In Malcolm's village, boys and girls made cricket bats from the wide end of the enormous coconut palm leaves.

A cricket pitch could easily be set up in any clear patch of ground and there were miles of sandy beaches. Everyone joined in the game. Fielders would swim out to sea to retrieve the ball and picnickers moved out of the line of fire.

These cricket matches lasted well into the fading sunset on many warm Caribbean evenings. Life was good in Trinidad.

CHAPTER FIVE

Family

RUDOLPH'S FATHER, RALPH, lived in Tunapuna, five miles from the village where Rudolph lived with his mother and two younger sisters.

Once a month, on a Friday night, his mother said, "Malcolm, here's the bus fare to Tunapuna. Go and get some money from Ralph." His mother never referred to his father by anything but his name.

Rudolph took the bus fare from his mother, but he always walked the five miles in the blazing hot sun, all the way to Tunapuna. He spent the bus fare on mauby, a popular, bittersweet drink and a rock cake.

His father usually gave him a few dollars for his mother and ten cents for himself. He never spent one penny on bus fares. He walked the five miles home.

Rudolph had a remarkable great aunt. Aunt Ada was his grandmother's sister. He loved her. He spent his holidays with her as a young boy. He went to her whenever he was in trouble and although she was always busy, she stopped work and listened to him.

She lived near Port of Spain, the capital city of Trinidad. She had a large, happy family. They had their meals in a big dining room where all the family gathered around two tables. It was here that Rudolph learned table manners.

Rudolph will always carry the memory of his aunt asking him three times if he had finished eating. After

answering, "Yes" for the third time, he realised that all the other children had their knives and forks neatly together on their plates and his were splayed out across his empty plate. He didn't know that he was supposed to close his knife and fork together to show that he had finished the meal. But he learned.

CHAPTER SIX

School Days

AT THE AGE OF SIX, Rudolph was sent to Barataria Church of England School. He loved it. He was popular with pupils and teachers alike.

He stayed at that school until he was sixteen. Rudolph excelled in arithmetic and was a whiz at poetry. In all the other subjects, he did just about enough to get by.

He made up lots of poems. With a pencil and exercise book in his pocket, Rudolph scribbled verse after verse. Sometimes he wrote far into the night, until his mother turned off the kerosene lamp and ordered him to bed.

The teachers liked his poems, and because he could recite them well, he was given top rating in the school drama group. He loved being on stage, even at that early age.

The school uniform was smart and with each success at school, Malcolm felt better about himself. With the passing years and growing confidence, he joined the cricket club at Barataria Elementary School. He practised hard and was soon the opening batsman for the team.

Even now, Rudolph plays cricket in England for The Bunbury's, a team that includes actors and other celebrities as well as England and West Indies cricket players. He has also played in cricket matches with other members of the *EastEnders* cast to raise money for a variety of charities.

At school, Rudolph also joined the football team because this kept him popular with his schoolmates, including the girls. His school days were very active indeed. However, all this prancing about wreaked havoc with his shoes.

There was very little money in the family and there were two younger sisters to feed and clothe also. Rudolph had only one pair of shoes.

One day, after a hectic football game at school and kicking a ball with his friends along the road home, his shoes split wide open, gaping at the front like a laughing mouth.

He limped miserably home, with his friends teasing him all the way.

"Malcolm, Malcolm, you have the blues!
Malcolm, Malcolm with the laughing shoes!"

His mother gave him a good telling off and a painful thwack on the back of his legs for ruining his only pair of shoes.

"I paid good money for those. I can't afford new

ones. You just have to manage, " she complained.

He went to bed and spent a sleepless night, hoping for a miracle. But, the next day, he limped along the road to school, trying to ignore the giggling girls. They pointed at his shoe, flopping around as he raised his left foot high in the air to keep from tripping himself up and falling flat on his face.

The remaining years at school were very ordinary. Further education meant having to pay fees and his mother could not afford to. So, at age 16, in 1954, Malcolm left school and went out to work.

Rudolph on his way to work
at the Government Printing Office

CHAPTER SEVEN

A Passion for Acting

HIS FIRST JOB was with the Government Printing Office as an apprentice with a printing company. He was barely interested in the job. He only managed to get through each day because he joined an amateur theatre group, the Company of Players, which he went to in the evenings. His career as an actor was beginning.

During these years in Trinidad, Rudolph became restless. He came to realise that on a small island, there was limited scope for his ambition to be an actor.

Rudolph with Errol John, in Trindidad in 1960

He asked the advice of many people inside and outside the world of acting. Some advised him to stay in the Caribbean and try and make his career there. Then one piece of advice changed his life forever.

A celebrated Trinidadian actor, Errol John, arrived in Trinidad from London. Errol's career had taken off in London and he was becoming known in Hollywood as well.

Rudolph sent an invitation to Errol to come and see him acting in the amateur group's staging of *The Story of the Robe,* a biblical play. To his surprise, Errol accepted the invitation and even stayed on after the play to chat with him.

The Story of the Robe,
Rudolph is in the middle
wearing the big helmet

"Pack your bags and go to England, Malcolm," Errol advised. "The training for actors there is far superior than in the USA."

Rudolph was delighted and could not wait to tell his mother.

But she was not impressed. "You have a good job at the printers. You could work up over the years to become a supervisor!" she said. "Why do you want to go to England? How do you know you could manage there?"

Rudolph was disheartened.

Then suddenly, a few days later, his mother said, "Look here, son, if you really want to go to England, then you should. You have my blessing."

Rudolph was shocked and absolutely delighted.

His mother borrowed the money from a local money lender and an old uncle found him a place to stay in London.

On the night of 20th August 1960, Rudolph waved goodbye to his family and friends and sailed out of Port of Spain for England on board the *Oranje Nassau*, a Dutch ocean liner. He was 20 years old.

CHAPTER EIGHT

England

HIS FIRST REAL EXPERIENCE of England was quite a shock.

At school in Trinidad, every one of Rudolph's text books was set in the British Isles. His history books told the history of England, from Richard the Conqueror, through the Tudors and Stuarts to the present. He learned science from books about Britain. In his biology books, the animals and plants were those of the cold, northern countries of the world, not of his tropical island home.

All his fiction, non-fiction and poetry books had white heroes. These books mostly showed the life of rich English people. With only information from books, Rudolph had imagined England very differently from what he saw when he arrived.

His ship docked at Southampton on a grey day. The train journey from the port to Waterloo Station in London gave him glimpses of rows upon rows of identical houses with a backdrop of a grey sky.

From the books Rudolph read all through his early life in the Caribbean, he gained the impression that all English people were well educated, well read and well off. So he was shocked to find poor people and even more shocked to find people who could not read!

His first London home was a bedsit five minutes from Dalston Market, among the not-so-privileged people of London. He lived in a cramped room in that cold damp house on a bleak street for four or five years.

His first priority was to earn money for food and rent. He found a job at Billington Press, a little print shop on the Kingsland Road.

On his way to work one day, he found himself walking beside a young woman.

"Hello! How are you? I'm new over here. Can I walk with you?" he asked in a gentle voice.

"Get away from me, or I will call the police!"

Rudolph turned and walked quickly in the opposite direction. This and other similar experiences taught him that people in London were not as friendly and relaxed as they were back home. It was not normal in this big, grey city to greet strangers in the street and start a conversation.

It became quite obvious to Rudolph that finding

friends, a place to live and a good job would prove difficult. In the newspapers, when he looked for a place to live, he found adverts for rooms which stated clearly, "No coloureds, no Irish, no dogs."

He refused to be put off by the unfriendly folk, the weather, the strange food, the small houses that were all close together. Rudolph found a focus.

He worked all day, every day, during the week and then prepared for his acting career by going to evening classes. He studied at the City Literary Institute in Holborn. It was excellent training. For two years he learned speech, mime, fencing, dancing and all the subjects which would help his career.

Northchurch Road, Rudolph's home in the 60s

CHAPTER NINE

Early Acting Days

IN ORDER TO GET WORK, actors sign up with agents. These agents actively search the acting world for jobs for their clients and they take a percentage of the wages paid to the actor.

In those days, there was only one black agent in London. Pearl Connor, a Trinidadian, worked tirelessly to place black actors in the theatre and on television. Pearl found Rudolph a walk-on, non-speaking part in a Saturday-night play on television.

The play was set in Africa. Rudolph was in most of the crowd scenes. He was so excited, he told all his friends and work colleagues about his TV role.

The house Rudolph lived in at that time was in Northchurch Road in Islington. It was a large house, divided into bedsits. The tenants were mainly people who had emigrated from the Caribbean. Rudolph told them all about his part in the play.

On the night the play was shown, instead of playing dominoes or draughts, they all gathered in one bedsit, in front of a small black and white television. They brought in food and drink and waited with excitement for the hour-long play to begin.

Fifteen minutes went by with not one on-screen sighting of Rudolph. After about half an hour with no appearance of their friend, remarks from the group began.

"You sure you are in this play?"

"Have we got the right date? The right time?"

Then suddenly, as they chatted, they caught a glimpse of Rudolph on the far edge of a large crowd scene. In the blink of an eye, he and the dead body he was carrying, had disappeared. There was one more close-up which lasted a second or two. That was it.

No-one had told Rudolph that with just a walk-on part, most of it would end up on the cutting room floor.

"What was that about?" asked one of his guests.

"One glimpse is what we were sitting here all this time for?"

"I blinked and missed him!" hissed another.

But it was all light hearted and soon forgotten.

Rudolph continued to play walk-on and small parts in theatre and crowd scenes on television. Then on Thursday, 19th September 1964, Rudolph had his first professional appearance on stage.

It was in an American play, *The Cave Dwellers*, by William Saroyan. Apart from Rudolph, the entire

Rudolph is on the right, as Jamie in *The Cave Dwellers*,
his first stage play in England

cast was white. The entire audience was white also.

Rudolph decided that he would have to work extremely hard to prove himself. Luckily, his boss at Billington Press agreed to let him have time off for rehearsals.

CHAPTER TEN

Rudolph on Stage

THAT SAME YEAR, *Fear of the Panther* by Jean McConnell, was staged at the Richmond Theatre in Surrey. Rudolph was delighted to work with two well-established black actors, Bari Johnson from Jamaica and Carmen Munroe from Guyana.

His director commented on the sheer vitality that he brought to the part. There was also negative criticism of his work, but Rudolph used that to help him to improve his technique.

Rudolph's first professional role in a classic play was as Othello, the main character in Shakespeare's play of the same name. This production ran successfully at the Malvern Festival Theatre in February 1966.

Othello is a black character. In those days, many directors argued that black actors could not be cast in important roles, because none of them had enough experience to perform such classics. They used 'blacked up' white actors in the roles instead.

Rudolph ignored this kind of negative thinking and the play had great reviews. His acting career was well on its way.

Rudolph as Othello at Malvern Festival Theatre
with Nerissa Knight as Desdemona

In February 1967 the talented producer Dr Jonathan
Miller placed him in *Benito Cereno*, a play by Robert
Lowell at the Mermaid Theatre, London. Jonathan
Miller had directed this play very successfully in the
United States before he brought it to the London
stage.

Acting alongside Rudolph were two black actors,
Norman Beaton (who starred in *Desmond's*) and
Nina Baden-Semper. Nina was to co-star with

Rudolph, a few years later, in the popular and long running television series *Love Thy Neighbour*.

Jonathan Miller was pleased with Rudolph's performance and later cast him twice in the role of Caliban in *The Tempest,* another Shakespeare play. Other Shakespearean parts played by Rudolph in theatre included the part of Friar Lawrence in *Romeo and Juliet* at the Young Vic in London in 1987. This play also went to Germany.

Rudolph as Caliban with Peter Bayliss
in *The Tempest*, at The Old Vic Theatre, London, 1988

In 1990, he was the narrator in *Pericles*, at the Royal Shakespeare Company, followed by the part of Flavius in *Timon of Athens*.

Sometimes there were periods when work was difficult to find. At other times, Rudolph dashed from playing *Othello* at the Young Vic in the afternoon, to the Tricycle Theatre in North London to appear in Mustapha Matura's *Playboy of the West Indies*.

He was supported by good advice from Earl Cameron, a Guyanese actor living and working in England at that time. He led younger actors by good example and told Rudolph that "praise does not mean you are perfect". Earl was always supportive when times were hard for younger actors.

CHAPTER ELEVEN

Rudolph Becomes a Star

RUDOLPH'S CAREER IN TELEVISION began with *On the Buses* in 1969.

After a few episodes had been recorded, he was dropped from the show. The series carried on with no black actors.

At the time, there was a high percentage of black people working on the buses as drivers and conductors for London Transport. They had been recruited specially from the Caribbean because of a shortage of staff in England. The show most certainly didn't reflect what was actually happening on the road in real life.

It was as Bill Reynolds in *Love Thy Neighbour* in 1970, that Rudolph became famous. This was a successful TV series. It propelled him into the limelight and made him a household name.

He began to be recognised. He was constantly greeted by people on the street and on trains and buses. Rudolph and the cast of *Love Thy Neighbour* became celebrities. Wherever they went they were swamped by fans.

Rudolph with fans of *Love Thy Neighbour*

Once, the whole cast was invited to a workers party at Vauxhall Motors in Luton. Many of the employees at Vauxhall were excited about this visit.

When the actors arrived in Luton, a large group of women broke away from the waiting crowd. They ran screaming hysterically, heading straight for Rudolph, shouting "Bill! Bill!" (the name of his character in the show). He had to be whisked away quickly by security guards and hidden in a marquee until they could control the fans.

Over four years, the BBC recorded 52 episodes of *Love Thy Neighbour*. In 1972 the TV actors took a stage version of the show to Australia on tour. The first stop was Melbourne. From Melbourne the tour moved to Sydney.

Another TV programme, *Black Silk* in 1984, was the series which Rudolph enjoyed most in his career. He liked playing Larry Scott, a barrister, because the character was engaging. Back then, it was also one of the few times that a black actor was central to the story and carried the plot.

The cast of *Love Thy Neighbour,* from the left,
Rudolph, Kate Williams, Nina Baden-Semper, Jack Smethurst

Rudolph's high profile as a well-known actor has allowed him to give support to the black community by doing charity work. He supports the African Caribbean Leukaemia Trust. He's also Patron of the Eastside Young Leaders Academy which "exists to nurture and develop the leadership potential of young African and Caribbean males, empowering them to become the next generation of successful leaders".

Rudolph visits a school

CHAPTER TWELVE
Life and Work

AN INTERVIEW WITH RUDOLPH WALKER:

Q: Do you enjoy your work?

A: Yes. Very much. It has given me – and I've been told, many others – great pleasure and brought many rewards.

Q: If you had not succeeded in becoming an actor, what would you have done?

R: I would have trained as a barrister, I think. It would have involved a great deal of performing... in court in front of the judge and jury!

Q: Do you go back to Trinidad where you were born?

R: Yes, at least twice every year. It's my way of keeping real. Back there, I'm Malcolm from the hood. I have a home there and go to relax, eat, see friends and family...

Q: How can someone get into acting?

R: Training is very important. The competition is great. It's also important to have real talent. I would advise going to a good drama school to have that talent challenged and stretched. There you can improve your acting, singing and dancing and learn all the things that help towards a successful career.

Q: Do you find learning lines easy?
A: Not at all. I work hard at learning them. I hate getting on the set without my lines firmly nailed in my head. Sometimes, though, I can be distracted and then we have to do re-takes. That's easy on television. On stage, however, there's only one take!

Q: Do you have to be white to get a leading role? For example, do you have to be white to play *Macbeth*?
A: No. You don't. Shakespeare's stories are written about love, hate, greed and all the elements that make up human behaviour. In any case, acting is pretending to be something that you are not!

CHAPTER THIRTEEN

Trinidadians of Note

IN ONE OF HIS SPEECHES in support of a London MP, Bernie Grant in 2002, Rudolph said, "Forty-three years ago, I embarked on a journey. It has taken me from San Juan on the beautiful island of Trinidad to Europe, America, Africa and Australia.

"But I am only following in the footsteps of a long line of great Trinidadian artists and icons who have left their mark on society. Among them are the late Edric Connor, actor and singer, Samuel Selvon

Rudolph with President A.N.R. Robinson of Trinidad and Tobago and his wife, and Sir Trevor McDonald, OBE

the famous writer, Horace James the actor and comedian, Errol John the actor, Winifred Atwell the great jazz singer and pianist, and more recently, V.S. Naipaul, Sir Trevor McDonald OBE, Sir Horace Ové and Floella Benjamin.

"This journey is littered with many ups and downs, disappointments, excitement, rejection and racism, but there have been many accolades and numerous successes as well. Throughout this journey, I have been Malcolm from Trinidad. That has held me on course throughout my acting career, from Bill Reynolds in *Love Thy Neighbour* in the 1970's, Larry Scott the sharp barrister in BBC's *Black Silk*, Grandpa Langley in *The Crouches* and Patrick Trueman in *EastEnders,* which is seen by 15 million viewers, four nights a week."

For his work as an actor Rudolph was awarded the Most Excellent Order of the British Empire (OBE) by the Queen in 2006. This is an honorary knighthood that is awarded to people who distinguish themselves in the arts, science and other areas of public life.

Photo Credits

p1: *EastEnders* : 2004 : Yolande and Patrick 01/01/2004 © BBC. Picture shows: ANGELA WYNTER as Yolande and RUDOLPH WALKER as Patrick Trueman. TX: Thursday 8th July 2004 Patrick and Yolande are awaiting a visit from the social worker to talk about their suitability for fostering. They play up plans for their imminent wedding and Yolande reveals her pain at not being able to have children. They impress the intervewer with their commitment but are thrown when the B&B is deemed an unsuitable environment for children.

p2: © BBC Adam Pensotti 2003. Picture shows: GARY BEADLE as Paul, RUDOLPH WALKER as Patrick and NICHOLAS R BAILEY as Dr Trueman. TX: BBC ONE Mondays, Tuesdays, Thursdays and Fridays

p3: *EastEnders* : 2005 : Patrick Trueman 17/08/2005 © BBC. Picture Shows: RUDOLPH WALKER as Patrick Trueman. Generic. First Appearance: 13.09.2001.

p4: *Black Silk* 01/01/1985 © BBC. Picture shows : Rudolph Walker as black barrister Larry Scott. Drama series about a black lawyer in London, devised by Mustapha Matura and Rudy Narayan.

p6: *EastEnders* : 2006 : Denise and Patrick *week 49 01/01/2006 © BBC. Picture shows: DIANE PARISH as Denise Wicks, RUDOLPH WALKER as Patrick Trueman. TX: BBC ONE Monday 4th December 2006 Denise apologises to Patrick - the matter with Aubrey is still preying on her mind. Patrick is full of guilt and admits to Denise that the test was negative - he's not her father...

p7: *EastEnders* : 2005 : Peggy, Patrick and Yolande 01/01/2005 © BBC. Picture Shows: BARBARA WINDSOR as Peggy Mitchell, RULDOLPH WALKER as Patrick Trueman and ANGELA WYNTER as Yolande. TX: Friday 4th November 2005 The grand opening of Patrick's car lot.

p30: The Cave Dwellers, 1st night, St Pancras Town Hall, 2 March, 1961. Photo by Russ Allen Ltd.

p32: Photo by Gerald Pates.

Thanks to Rudolph Walker for use of his personal photos.

Every effort has been made to trace any copyright owners of the photos in this book and people who appear in the photos and to reference their sources. Where any permissions have proved unobtainable then the publishers will be pleased to hear from the owners and will be glad to correct any inaccuracies as they deem appropriate.

OTHER TAMARIND TITLES

BLACK STARS

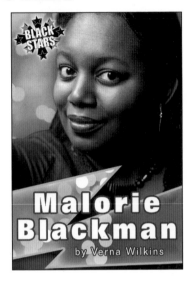

Tamarind readers

www.tamarindbooks.co.uk